This Book Belongs To

_____

Rescued!
The Amazing Story of Gertie Agouti

By Dwain Lovett and Marcia Mitchell
Photography By Dwain Lovett

ISBN: 978-1-942333-10-4

Performance Strategies Publishing

A Family of Three

Have y'all ever heard of an Agouti?

Me neither, and I'm a great big dog from Texas who knows a lot about life. That is, I *thought* I knew most everything until this amazin' agouti business happened.

Before we get into all the amazin' stuff, y'all need to know somethin' about me and my family. Right up front, I'll tell you I'm not some kinda ranch dog who does stuff like fool around with horses and cowboys. No sir, I'm a swimmin', ball playin', varmint chasin' dog, and I have a big soft heart. Dontcha let on that you know that last part. I'd be embarrassed cuz I'm s'posed to be a big, tough guy. And I am, most of the time.

I didn't know beans about agoutis until the three of us, Mom, Dad, and me, moved to this island in the Caribbean called Montserrat. I had to look at a map to even see where a place like that could be. (I threw that map in the back of the book for y'all.) And then, wow, we learned a whole bunch about agoutis.

Well, pardon me, but I plum forgot to introduce myself. My name is K-Pax. My friends call me Pax.

I need to tell y'all about my family. I love this family more'n a dog loves bein' lost in a meat market. I came to live with them when I was only eight weeks old and not even knee-high to a Texas grasshopper.

Two nice lookin' people came to where I was born to find a new puppy. I had seven brothers and sisters, so we were all scramblin' to look adorable so's we could get adopted.

They seemed like mighty nice people, and they had a great big dog with them. He was an old coot named Picard, a Yellow Lab like me. I guess he was s'posed to help them choose the right puppy. Anyhow, I could tell right away he didn't have use for any of us. Nope. He liked bein' an only dog.

As soon as the lady came to where all us puppies were, I up and scooted over and plopped down on her foot. It was too soon. She wanted to look at all the other puppies and let that snooty lookin' Picard make the choice. I hoped I didn't blow my chance by bein' so pushy.

Well, like I said, Picard didn't want any of us. He just walked around all uppity and ignored us all.

That was when I saw my chance! I went right over and sat on that lady's foot again. I wiggled a little and tried real hard at bein' adorable. It musta worked, cuz she reached down and picked me up. She smiled and said, "Well, this must be the right one."

I got to sit in the lady's lap all the way home. That's when I knew she was my Mom. Lemme tell y'all, I was happier'n all get-out.

My new house was within spittin distance of a lake. I got to go swimmin' a lot, and that was fun. I even learned how to play ball.

The folks who lived next door were Grandma and Grandpa to Picard and me. They would take us for walks every day, rain or shine.

It was Grandpa who taught me how to play ball. He'd throw it and I would run fast as greased lightning. I'd get that ball and bring it right back to him. I could do that all day long.

I already told y'all that Picard was an old coot, and he was, but he was a smart old coot. I learned a lot from him. Listenin' and learnin' from him made me a real smart dog. You can learn a lot by listenin' to older folks.

We had a great life in Texas, good food and lotsa land. Then one day Mom and Dad told me we was movin' to Montserrat. I didn't know where that was, but they said there was lotsa water and I could swim as much as I wanted. I was ready and rarin' to go!

Before we could hit the road, I had to learn how to be a service dog. That way, I could ride on the airplane with them and not be stuck in a crate down below, like some ordinary dog. Dad was told he had a sickness that would mess up his hands, so I got to learn how to help him do things.

Learnin' to be a service dog was hard work, but bein' smart like I am, it was easy as fallin' off a log.

Picard decided to stay in Texas and keep Grandma and Grandpa company. He was happy he was gonna be an only dog again.

This place called Montserrat is prettier'n a sunset over a barbeque. There's lotsa funny lookin' trees they call palms. They're skinnier'n a gnat's whisker and look like they're carryin' umbrellas.

When we got to our new house, I saw there was a little lake right inside the house— just for me to swim in. Mom called it a pool, and told me I could swim in it anytime I wanted. How cool is that?

Mom, Dad, and I have a great time. We take walks, go swimmin' and we go to the beach a lot. I love the beach. You gotta be careful of the waves though, cuz they'll knock you down and roll you over. Don't ever go in the ocean without a pal, just in case.

Everything is hunky-dory for our family of three, and then one day they say we're gettin' a cat. "What in the dickins? You have me, what else could y'all possibly want?"

Mom said she was scared of mice and rats and she wanted a cat to keep them away. Okay, I figure it's all right with me. I sure don't wanna be the one chasin' after those things.

So, we go to this place and there's a tiny cat in a box. She looks real sleepy. I give her a good smellin' over and tell Mom she is okay with me.

Now that we have a cat, that makes us a family of four. In order of size, it's Dad, Mom, me, and the cat. I kinda like havin' a critter smaller 'n me around, lets her know who's in charge 'round here.

A Tiger Comes To Stay

I am the cat! You will soon learn that I am also the heroine in this story—not Pax, not Mom, not Dad. *Moi*. That's how you say "me" in French.

My name is Jasmine, but my Dad calls me "Princess." I tried to tell him that "Your Royal Highness" would be more appropriate, but Mom says I would have to get approval from Her Majesty the Queen of England before I can be called that. This is a British island, after all. Thus, my dears, you may call me "Jazz." Dad tells me that I am named after a tiger in a movie. I find that quite fitting.

I am tough as nails, but *extremely* sophisticated. You will never hear me using improper language, as Pax sometimes does. And I never say "meow," although I do use "mew" on occasion. I am quite small for a cat, slender and graceful. In fact, it has been said that I move with the grace of a tiger. Isn't that what one would expect from a heroine?

I first met Pax, Mom, and Dad when they came to visit me in the doctor's office. I was resting up there after being ill. They looked like a nice couple and had with them an extremely large yellow dog. He looked me over as if I were a diamond he was contemplating buying. I was nervous, but his kindly manner led me to believe that he was not about to hurt me. He told me his name was K-Pax, but that his friends called him Pax.

It was clear that Pax's approval of me pleased Mom and Dad. So it was settled, and I went home with them to live in this beautiful house by the sea.

As for this new Mom and Dad, I think I can train them to be just what I want them to be. It is *so* important for a cat to train the humans with whom she lives. Mine are kind and treat me very well, which is what I deserve. They have a nice house, lovely places to nap, and plenty to eat. Mom says that I am to keep mice and rats away from the house. A perfect assignment for this tiger!

I am a Montserratian cat. Montserratian cats talk a lot and talk loudly. We understand it's important to let others know what is wanted. Fortunately, Mom and Dad learned quickly, and from our first day together they behaved beautifully.

I get to roam the neighborhood whenever I want, day or night. These excursions are necessary if I'm going to mark my territory, which is very important to a well-bred cat.

Life in my new neighborhood is grand, except for some ill-tempered, large cats who enjoy starting fights. They are a lot bigger than me and, tough as I am, there have been times when I needed a helping paw.

There was something those cats did not know. Not only am I strong, but I am also very, very fast. If one of those mean, bigger cats became too hard to handle, I would run away and head for home. The bully cat would chase me the whole way.

Now comes the absolutely fabulous part. When I got close to home, I would call, "Pax, Pax," and he would come running, appearing and sounding ferocious.

Did I mention that Pax is huge? I mean HUGE!

It was absolutely glorious to see the look on a mean cat's face when he saw Pax tearing at him full speed! Skidding to a stop, the foolish feline would turn around and head across the street to climb the nearest mango tree. I found it all very amusing. More amusing would have been my chasing the cat up the tree and teaching it a lesson. But, I must allow Pax a bit of fun, too.

After the chase, Pax would come to check on me, sniffing and rolling me over with his nose, making sure I was okay. I couldn't have imagined a dog treating a cat so kindly, but that is what big brothers are for, after all.

When I'm working, I hunt for mice, birds, rats, snakes, and lizards. I bring them into the house so everyone can see what an expert I am at my job. Mom complains when I bring live mice inside. It seems she doesn't approve of me playing with my food. When I bring in a mouse, she lets out an ear-piercing scream.

Of course her biggest scream was not about a mouse.

Abandoned

Me name be Gertie and me love me new family. Me a Montserrat agouti. Me speak Montserrat Creole Dialect. That's a language from a long time ago that mix up English and African languages.

"Me no know" means "I don't know" in English. Me use "me" a lot instead of "I" like most people do. Jazz tells me that me must learn the Queen's English like her. I do try, but me still mix 'em up sometime. Most of de time, actually.

How did me come to live with dis family? The first thing me remember is being moved from the burrow where me be born out into the bush and then left all by meself. Where was me agouti family?

It be very dark, and me feel very strange. Me eyes be barely open and me very, very scared. Where me mommy be? Where is me family? I try to move, but me front legs is mash up. I smell de grass, so me nose be working. Oh, me so scared!

Me see something move in de grass. Me mommy? No, it's a big thing with stripes and round gold and yellow eyes. It come close and start to smell me. Is it going to eat me? Me just lay there and shiver. I think, "please don't let this thing eat me!"

"I am a tiger," it says. "Tigers are quite special."

Next thing me know, the tiger has me in its mouth and is carrying me away. I ride in dat tiger's mouth a long way from the burrow where me be born. Then, me be dropped on something hard. De tiger no eat me. It jus' sit there and look at me. Maybe he bring me back to me agouti family.

Den me hear a terrible sound. "A rat! Kill it, kill it!"

What kinda agouti make a sound like dat?

Der be a lotta noise, and den some kinda big animal with only two legs pick me up. Is it the one who be going to eat me? Mebbe not. De big animal is gentle and kind. It rub me fur and me little heart quit pounding so hard.

Me wish me could see better, but me eyes be barely open. After all, me only one day old.

Dis really big animal carry me in he hand, and den he put me back into some high grass in de bush. Mebbe me not going to be eaten—at least not yet! Mebbe me mommy come find me now. Me hope so. Me hungry.

Me should be able to take care of meself, but me can't, because me front legs be mash up. Me lost and very scared all alone. Den it gets dark, so me lay down to sleep.

Me wakes up when de grass starts moving and me know something come near me again. Me try to keep very quiet so mebbe it no see me.

It de tiger come back! Oh me! It pick me up by de back of me neck and carry me like before. What kind of tiger is dis? Does it wants to help me? Maybe it know where me can find some food.

After carrying me a long time, de tiger jump through a hole and we inside a big cave with all kinds of strange things in it. Den de tiger lay me down on de same kind of hard ground like before, and lay down to watch me. Me no know what to think. So me just go back to sleep. Me just a baby you know.

Suddenly, me hear a noise. Something coming! It's de big two-legged animal again, and this time with a huge yellow creature. De huge yellow creature sniff me all over, but do not hurt me. De two-legged one pick me up very gently and say something about jasmine. De tiger come up and just look at de two-legged animal what hold me. De tiger calls the big animal "Dad" and tells him, "I want to keep her."

De Dad say, "Okay Jasmine, if you want to keep her, I guess we have to."

Do dis mean me not gonna be eaten?

What's the Big Deal?

Look, I found something in the woods and decided I wanted to keep it. What's the big deal? I thought about what to do with it, and decided that I wanted to keep it rather than put it on my menu for the day. Who would have guessed that my decision would end up making me famous?

If "the something" had been a rat, I would have brought it home to play with until I got tired of it and then put it out of its misery. I would have left it in the dining room for Mom to find, as I do with mice. She gets really hysterical when I do that.

Here's my personal view of what happened: I was out hunting one day and decided to take a look in the woods near my home. I heard a chirping sound and thought I had found a bird to have for lunch. It seemed like a good idea, especially because I hadn't had a bite to eat since breakfast.

I crept up slowly, tiger-like, until I saw that it was not a bird after all. It was a baby agouti! This surprised me, because I know every inch of my neighborhood and I know everyone who lives here, which certainly does not include a family of agoutis. I sniffed the baby and it didn't move. "Where is its mother?"

Upon inspecting further, I saw that the baby's front legs seemed to be misshapen. Hmmm. I could put it out of its misery and maybe have it for lunch. It looked as if it would be tasty.

Now, this is one of the amazing parts of the story. I can't explain why, but I did not want to hurt the little thing. Something about doing so just did not seem right. Still, I am a hunter, and I found myself wondering why I felt so different about this tiny creature. Never mind. For whatever reason, I liked this baby. I thought perhaps I should take it home and keep it.

So I did! I picked it up by the scruff of the neck, took it home and put it on the tile floor in my dining room. Poor thing just lay there. I felt so sorry for it.

Remember how Mom screams when she sees a mouse or rat? You should have heard this one! Then Dad came in with a plastic bag to get rid of the baby, just like he always does with the mice and rats I leave for Mom.

"It's a newborn agouti," Dad says, then adds that he cannot hurt it. Mom is out on the verandah saying, "Kill it! Kill it!" But Dad will not. He takes the baby agouti out back and gently places it in the tall grass. He tells the baby that it should be with its mother in a burrow in the ground, where baby agoutis are supposed to stay for months.

Did I mention how very wise I am? I knew something was wrong. I certainly did not see a mother out there in the grass. And, I wondered, did the mother leave the baby on its own because it was different? Because it had legs that did not work? That would be a terrible thing to do. I watch, making a very clever plan.

After Mom and Dad retire to bed that night, I go into the tall grass and find the baby agouti. It is scared to death, surely thinking it is about to be eaten. I gently pick it up again, being extra careful not to hurt it, and head for home. I take the baby back inside my house through the louver window—which is my entrance when they close all the doors. It is a little tricky, because the agouti is heavier than a mouse or rat, and I have to be careful not to hurt it.

I put the little agouti right in the path that Dad and Pax take every morning to get breakfast. I am nothing if not subtle. Then I sit back and wait.

Sure enough, Dad and Pax come in and see the baby. Will Dad understand that I want to keep it? I certainly hope I have trained him well enough.

I am not moving, just sitting quietly and giving him my most serious stare.

Dad picks the baby up and looks at me. He says to Pax, "Well, I guess Jazz wants to keep this baby agouti." Then Dad says, "Okay Jasmine, if you want to keep her, I guess we have to."

Yes! I have trained him well.

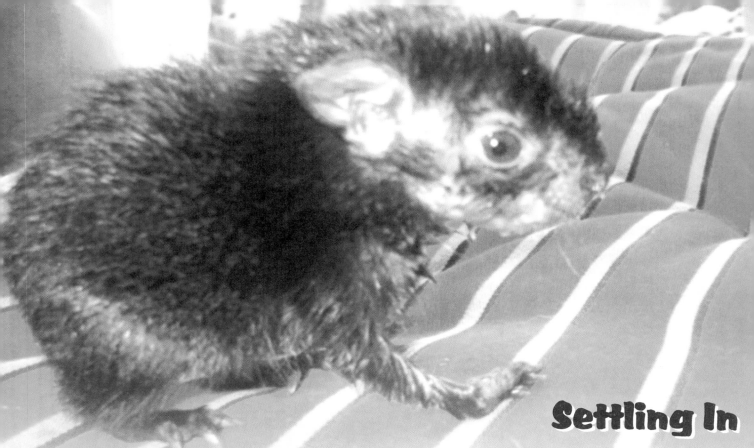

Settling In

De Dad get a box and put me into it. Me be quiet and listen to everybody chirping. Maybe dis going to be okay after all. Me learn dat de tiger am a cat name Jasmine and dat me really lucky to be in a box and not in her tummy. De other animal is called dog and be named Pax. De two-legged animal be "Dad."

Me hear another sound, dis one from a different two-legged animal, one much prettier dan de Dad animal. Her lean over and look in me box. De Dad, he say, "Jazz brought the agouti back into the house through the window, so I guess we have to keep it."

De pretty one be "Mom." She bring me a banana to eat. She hold it for me because me front legs be mash up. Dat okay with me, because agoutis hold food with forepaws to eat, like a squirrel do. Sometime me get banana all over me face. Dad take a picture of me face covered with banana.

Me like de Mom animal. She be very kind and gentle. She make me a bed and put it in a little room dat feel safe. She call it a "shower," and me wonder why dey call it a shower.

Me comfy here, but it be very different from de bush nearby where me born!

Mom bring some water to me. She say to Dad, "I'm using an eyedropper." It take me a little while to learn how to drink from it, but Mom, she say me a quick learner.

De cat comes in and say me talk like some of de Montserratians who mix English with local talk. She say it be pretty talk, but me now live with Americans and me should learn they talk. She say me should begin by saying "I" instead of "me" alla time. She say I should try to talk like her. See, me trying. Me mean, "I'm" trying.

This is getting to be fun. I get all the fruit and vegetables I can eat. In fact me can never eat it all, but me try.

Den one day Mom bring me white water she call "milk" and give me some with the eyedropper. It taste good, but now I can't poop. Agouti poop be little dry pellets and not messy at all. We be lucky dat way, but me no feeling lucky when no can poop. What me going to do? Being a good Mom, she sees that there is no poop to clean up and she gives me what she say be prune juice. It taste real good. And it makes me poop—a lot. Me hope der be no more milk.

Before long, I fit right in with the rest of the family and Jazz said I'm speaking better English, sometimes. Me spend most of me time in the shower in the bathroom, where me has plenty to eat and a cozy box to sleep meself in. Oh dear, Me still mix 'em up me language.

Mom and Dad take me out to talk to me and pet me. Dad tries to make me bad leg work right, but me no know if it will ever work right. It is all mash up. On me other leg me paw is mash up, too. It bends back and makes me walk on the back of me paw. But me no care. I hop around anyhow. Jazz and me play chase and hide-and-seek.

When me hiding, Mom asks Jazz, "Where is Gertie?" Jazz turns and looks to where I hiding and she give away me hiding place. Jazz watches over me like she me mommy.

I get to run loose in the house and explore. But soon me goes back into me bedroom and into my box to sleep and hide. I jump over a tall ledge to get into my bedroom. Me little, but me now able to hop on de ledge with one hop and into me room. Dad says that is amazing. He is proud of what me can do.

Me have plenty things to chew on, but me house I like the best. Mom says it is cardboard. Okay, but me like chewing it best of all. Then dey bring-a me a bigger box that has a hole in the front so me go inside to be safe. Me take me food inside for to hide and eat later.

Me hear Mom and Dad talking. Mom say, "How long will Gertie want to stay with us? When she grows older and stronger, will she want to be in the bush again, like other agoutis? Or will she want to stay with us and be a part of our family?"

Dad say, "We'll just have to wait and see. We can't send her out there until and unless she can take care of herself."

Me wonders what the answer will be. But me happy. Me like living here. I have a room all to meself and a place to sleep anytime me wants. Mom and Dad bring me food to eat and Jazz even comes in to see me. Sometimes me fall asleep curled up against Jazz and her give me a little kiss and let me stay there. And Mom and Dad do lots of holding and cuddling.

Life with me people family be much better than being in the bush. What would it be like to live in the woods with me agouti family? Do they miss me? Will I ever see them? What happens if I never see them? Could me stay alive jus by meself in de bush?

Me think about dem things, but now me really like it here with Jazz, Pax, Mom, and Dad. Me be safe and never worry about where to find food.

Me left front leg still no working good. Me right front paw, it still work backwards. But me don't let it keep me from doing what me want to do. Me learn to eat from food on the ground, insteada holding it in my front paws like other agoutis. Mom taught me to eat without using me paws by holding food for me to eat.

I like living in the house. I can even jump into my bedroom by myself. It is really high but me a very good jumper. My back legs work jus fine and I can hop very well. I say if one part doesn't work, just make your other part work better.

Jazz and I play in the house. I jump around and she follows me. It's fun. Pax doesn't like to play. He likes to take naps. Me glad he doesn't chase me—that would be scary!

I can feel that I am getting stronger. Ever since the prune juice thing, I have been eating and pooping like an agouti should. Me sleep a lot, but dey say that's what little ones do. I get plenty of exercise by hopping around my bedroom and playing with Jazz. And my language is getting better every day.

Me a very happy agouti. Oops! *I* am a very happy agouti.

A Family of Five

Things are perkin' right along havin' this new member of our family. When I first saw Gertie I was wonderin' what we were doin' with her. Funny how feelings change about someone who's different, once you get to know 'em up close.

So, here's the way I see the story:

The first time I laid eyes on Gertie I was on the way to get my breakfast. Dad and I do that every mornin'. So, here we are, trottin' in to rustle up some grub, and this little ball o' fur is right there on the floor. I sorta skid to a stop, cuz I guard the place and nobody's told me nothin' about a livin', breathin' ball o' fur.

I sniff the little bit of fluff, and she smells like nothin' I'd ever smelled before. Dad calls her an agouti and says that Jazz has brought her in and we're gonna keep her. Well, okay, as long as she doesn't get in the way of my breakfast dish.

These guys, agoutis, are like funny lookin' bunnies with round ears and long, pointy noses. Their back legs are way too long, so they look like they're runnin' downhill all the time. Kinda silly if you ask me. They're not really rabbits, but people who live on the island call them rabbits.

Dad says agoutis are in the guinea pig family, but I don't think they're close enough to send each other Christmas cards.

Dad named the agouti Gertie. He likes doing stuff like that. Gertie and Agouti just sounded good together. He named me after a movie about a planet. He named my big brother after the guy on Star Trek, Picard. He likes outer-space things. I didn't reckon this agouti that Jazz found came from outer space, but she could have.

Gertie fits right in with the rest of the family. She spends most of her time in the shower of the main bathroom. She has a box to sleep in and plenty of food to eat. She can move pretty good, even though her front legs are kinda messed up.

Mom and Dad take her out to pet her and talk to her. I'm embarrassed to say it, but even I try talkin' to her when nobody's lookin.' She always gives me a squinty sorta look that says, "Me no speak Texan." What kinda good English is that? She sounds to me like some of the Montserratian friends Mom and Dad have over for dinner. They speak a mix-up of local language and really snazzy English like Jasmine uses. Maybe I can teach Gertie some "Texanese."

Dad tries hard to make her left leg work like it is s'posed to. He tells her that it is "physical therapy." She doesn't like it one bit, because it kinda hurts her leg to have it moved forward to where it is s'posed to be.

Never you mind her having legs that don't work the way they're s'posed to. Gertie manages to run around the house and play just fine. She and Jazz play chase and hide-and-seek. Talk about cat and mouse games! It's like a doggone rodeo sometimes. The neighbors even come to watch. Other folks start callin' and askin' if they can come see the baby agouti and the cat. And they like to see me too, 'course. I get my picture took when Gertie gets up close while I'm nappin'. She's about the size of my paw, so visitors get a kick outta seeing us together.

When Gertie's runnin' loose, she explores the house, but soon goes back into the bathroom and the shower we call Gertie's bedroom. I reckon she feels at home there. She can even jump up onto the ledge in the shower door and hop into the shower—I mean her bedroom.

The ledge goin' into the shower is six inches high and six inches wide. Gertie's only four inches long, but she can hop up on the ledge with one jump and then over into her bedroom. That's like Dad jumpin' up onto the roof of our house!

Gertie weighed 5.6 ounces when she was just about one week old. Dad says an agouti named Flo, born in a zoo in Germany, weighed 4.6 ounces when she was three weeks old. Lemme tell y'all, our agouti, even with her leg problems, has done better'n Flo. We think

Gertie's fur is much nicer than Flo's, too. But then, we could be kinda biased cuz we love our agouti. Yep, I love her now, too. She's a part of our family, different or not.

So now we're a family of five. In order of size, it's Dad, Mom, me, Jazz, and Gertie. Jazz is glad to have someone smaller'n her in the family.

Growing Up

I have suggested to Mom and Dad that Gertie Agouti is an outside animal and needs a proper place in which to spend time out-of-doors. But she still must be protected and safe. I know. What I recommended is something easier said than done.

Mom does take her out of the house and lets her run in the grass. Mom backs away and the baby chases after her. It's good exercise and good fun; however, it is not enough.

Gertie needs more outside time than that. Perhaps she could have a shelter that gives her room to hop around in and still be protected.

I asked Pax for his opinion, and he suggested a playpen made of two-by-fours with a soil sifter—that's a net made of wire—for a roof. He knew Dad had one of those and it could work for a little while. She would be protected, would have fresh air, and could hop around in the grass. It would be especially nice if it were in the shade—maybe under some Elephant Ear plants. That way I could still check on her.

Gertie liked the idea. It was not fancy; but then, living in the bush in a burrow dug into the ground and lined with leaves, sticks, and hair is not exactly living in a fancy hotel either.

It worked for a little while, but Gertie was growing too fast for it to work for long. Then one day, Dad and Pax went to the hardware store. (Pax goes everywhere with Dad. He loves car rides.) They bought thirty feet of one-inch by one-inch mesh wire fencing, and in less than a day Gertie had a proper playpen. She seems to like it because she has lots of hopping room, fresh air, and room to exercise. Actually it is quite posh.

It was designed only for daytime use. She would continue to spend nights inside, sleeping in her bedroom. When she is outside, I, of course, sit beside the playpen and watch her.

Then, one day Mom looked for Gertie in her playpen, but she was not there. Mom got worried and shouted, "Where could she be?"

Mom and Dad looked all around. Pax even helped. Did Gertie get out and run away? And how did she get out? I sat very quietly and didn't mew a word.

Mom had a thought. She said out loud, "I know it isn't possible, but…," then she ran into the house. I got up and followed her. Mom looked into Gertie's bedroom, and there was the baby—sound asleep. "How could this happen?" Mom asks.

Dad comes in from outside and says he found the tiniest of holes under the fence, but, "How did she get into the house," he wondered. There were steps and ledges she could never manage.

Dad looks at me and says, "Look at Princess Cat. She's got guilt written all over her face."

Mom looks at me and says, "Jazz discovered the baby outside the playpen and carried her inside to her bedroom! This is amazing! Who in the world would believe this?"

I do not know what the fuss was about. I simply put the baby to bed for a nap.

Amazin'

Mom still takes Gertie out durin' the day for runs in the grass. She follows Mom around and has a lot of fun.

One day, Gertie hopped the other direction, away from Mom. I couldn't believe my eyes. She went straight to the veranda steps, which are eight inches tall. Gertie is about six inches tall by now. I'm figurin' no way Gertie makes it up the steps.

Wrong! She hopped right up the three steps. She slipped once, but bein' downright courageous and bullheaded, she tried again and made it. Mom and Dad looked like they couldn't believe it. In fact, that's just what Dad said. "I can't believe my eyes."

So what do you think Gertie did next? She hopped right into the living room and, without missin' a beat, made a beeline for the bathroom and into her bedroom. She cleared the ledge to the shower in a single leap and right into her cardboard house.

Now *that* is especially amazin'!

Gertie's right forepaw is okay now. She doesn't have to walk on the back of her paw anymore, and the sore spot is all healed up. Mom made a brace for her out of gauze and some special tape. Gertie's friend Rudolph, who looks after all of Mom 'n Dad's animal family, made the suggestion, and it worked. It made Gertie use her paw the right way, and now she can hop even better.

Our family sure wishes there was somethin' that could be done about Gertie's other front leg. She does use it for balance when she's runnin', but that's about it. At times she almost brings it all the way to the front, but it always goes backward to her left side. Seems that's how it is gonna be from now on.

But you know what? Gertie is okay with it and so are we. We all love her just the way she is.

Unconditional Acceptance

My decision to save Gertie's life certainly was serendipitous. She has become an important member of our family and is doing very well indeed. I would guess no other agouti in the world lives with a human family the way our Gerti does.

Gertie has become a celebrity. How did that happen? Who knows? Who cares? It just happened. And isn't that marvelous?

Dad sends reports on the Montserrat volcano to people who don't live on the island, so they know what is happening with the volcano. Occasionally, he includes other things that he thinks people might find of interest. A ferocious cat (yours truly) rescuing an abandoned agouti seemed like something interesting. And, so it was. Now Gertie has a fan club, and people all over the world want to know about her! As Pax would say, "How cool is that?"

Wherever Mom and Dad go, people ask, "How is Gertie?" At a party at the Governor's house, the first question the Governor asked was about Gertie. It is quite unusual, come to think of it. People do not usually greet each other by asking, "How is your cat?" or "How is your dog?"

We all realize that we have a great responsibility as the guardians of Gertie Agouti. But we believe that what we did—and are doing—is worthwhile. Gertie was saved from certain death in the bush and we, Mom, Dad, Pax and I, were chosen to keep her alive and help her grow up. It is our job to accept her just as she is.

Gertie is now up to 7.6 ounces in weight and getting longer. She's not a baby anymore, but at times she still depends on Mom to help her eat. One day Gertie picked up a whole mango by herself and carried it off to eat in private! Every day, she is learning more about taking care of herself. We all think Gertie could out-jump Flo at the German zoo any day of the week.

Gertie also likes singing a lot. It may not sound like singing to you, but you have to learn agouti language to know that it is singing. It sounds a bit like a bird chirping when she is happy and having a good time. Then sometimes she sounds a little like a dog growling. That is her warning voice used to scare off someone who might hurt her.

Gertie lives outside all of the time now, and likes it better that way. She has many friends who come to see her. Chickens that run wild in the neighborhood come visit her, and a lizard lives in the playpen with her. I check on her every day and watch over her. *Life is good!*

That's pretty much Gertie's story. Helpless, she was rescued and protected by a regal cat, a great big dog, and two human beings. All of us accepted her for who and what she is, just as she accepted us. We didn't mind that she was different from us, and she didn't mind that we were different from her. She learned to jump and hop and do lots of things despite having front legs that didn't work right.

Gerti proved she could overcome and accept imperfections in herself. Pax thinks that's terribly important. And you know what? I agree with him.

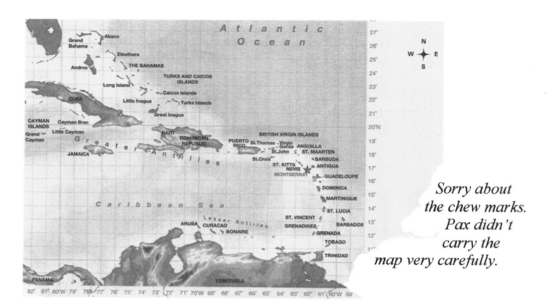

Sorry about the chew marks. Pax didn't carry the map very carefully.

A Few Facts About Agoutis

The amazing story of Gertie Agouti takes place on the small Caribbean island of Montserrat in the village of Old Towne. Montserrat happens to have an active volcano. It also happens to have agoutis.

Here's the big question: How did agoutis get to Montserrat in the first place? No one really knows, but scientists think these small creatures didn't travel alone. One guess is that agoutis came north from South America with the Arawak and Carib Indians, who moved up the East Caribbean island chain. It is likely the Indians brought agoutis along for food, not as dinner companions, but to eat. This happened a very long time ago. Agoutis look a little like rabbits, but with round ears and long, pointed noses. Many people living in the islands even call them rabbits, but they aren't really rabbits. Agoutis are in the Guinea Pig family.

These small animals are rodents who make their homes in the rainforests of Central and South America as well as in the Caribbean islands. The agoutis that live on Montserrat are Brazilian agoutis, *Dasyprocta leporine*, to be scientifically exact. Now you know their *genus* and *species*.

Agoutis are *nocturnal*, meaning they are night travelers. But on Montserrat, they can be seen foraging for food during the day. Serious about romance, they mate for life, and make their homes on the forest floor. Good planners, they bury their extra nuts and seeds in the **ground for later. If they get busy and forget about what they've buried, their stored nuts and seeds will make new trees in the rainforests.**

Did you wonder how Gertie could eat fruit right after she was born? Agoutis are *precocial*. This means they are able to do a lot on their own soon after being born. Baby chicks are another example of precocial animals. A healthy baby agouti may be up, around and eating within an hour after birth. That's being precocial!

In litters of two to four babies, agoutis are born in a burrow lined with leaves, roots, and hair. Their mothers give birth after three months of gestation. Agoutis can live as long as twenty years.

Agoutis are very fast runners, and can jump six feet straight up into the air. They can also turn 180° mid-air before coming down—a trick that's especially handy if they are in danger.

One of the things that makes Gertie's story so amazing is that agoutis are terribly shy by nature. They usually disappear in a hurry if they see other animals or human beings approaching. Even on Montserrat, seeing an agouti out in the open is very rare and certainly exciting! As for Gertie, nature might tell her it isn't appropriate for her to be cuddling in a human being's arms, or snuggling up close with a cat for a nap, but that is exactly what she wants to do.

Gertie, like all agoutis, loves nuts. Agoutis have such strong jaws, and their teeth are so sharp they can even open Brazil nuts, which have extremely hard shells. To help keep her teeth sharp, Gertie's new family makes certain that she has things to chew on.

Almonds grow wild on Montserrat and are one of Gertie's favorite menu items. She loves eating the outside, fleshy part of almonds. Not many people know it, but almonds are in the peach family. Crack open the pit next time you eat a peach and look at what's inside. It looks a lot like an almond, but don't try to eat it! It is really bitter.

While Gertie enjoys eating what other agoutis eat, she does have a taste for the unusual. Jasmine has a habit of not eating all of her wet cat food. After it dries out, she demands a fresh batch. Gertie found some of the dried-out bits and thought they tasted just fine. The problem is that agoutis are vegetarians. Since cat food has meat in it, she's not supposed to have it as part of her diet. Gertie was just curious and wanted to share a meal with Jazz. She doesn't eat Jazzy food anymore.

Curious, and fearless, Gertie was able to become close to a human family, a cat and a dog. She is changing a lot of minds about agoutis and teaching us things people never knew before. Things you now know!

About the Authors

Dwain Lovett was a long-time business development professional in the health care field while living in Texas. Dwain left Texas and his career and moved to the idyllic Caribbean island of Montserrat with Ruthann, his beautiful wife, and Pax, his big Yellow Labrador Retriever. Soon after arriving they added an arrogant island cat named Jasmine. Dwain enjoys being active in community activities and siestas in his hammock. The family's daily, uneventful lives changed dramatically when Gertie made her unexpected arrival.

Marcia Mitchell was a senior executive at the Corporation for Public Broadcasting and retired as associate director of the American Film Institute. An award-winning writer, she has published five non-fiction books and recently turned to fiction with the Maggie Sachet mysteries, called the "new must-read series for mystery fans." Marcia is also the author of the comedy, *What's Up, Pussycats*. Like so many others, Marcia fell in love with Amazing Gertie at the first cuddle. She divides her time between her homes in the Black Hills of South Dakota and on the island of Montserrat.

This book was selected for the Books 4 Kids Program
for its entertaining look at compassion and acceptance!

Visit www.B4KProgram.org to learn more about
Dwain Lovett, Marcia Mitchell and the
Books 4 Kids Program!